VEGETABLES
on MyPlate

by Mari Schuh

Consulting editor: Gail Saunders-Smith, PhD

Consultant: Barbara J. Rolls, PhD
Guthrie Chair in Nutrition
Pennsylvania State University
University Park, Pennsylvania

D1406557

CAPSTONE PRESS
a capstone imprint

Pebble Plus is published by Capstone Press,
1710 Roe Crest Drive, North Mankato, Minnesota 56003.
www.capstonepub.com

Library of Congress Cataloging-in-Publication Data
Schuh, Mari C., 1975–
   Vegetables on myplate / by Mari Schuh.
      p. cm.—(Pebble plus. What's on myplate?)
   Includes bibliographical references and index.
   Summary: "Simple text and photos describe USDA's MyPlate tool and healthy vegetable choices
for children"—Provided by publisher.
   ISBN 978-1-4296-8743-0 (library binding)
   ISBN 978-1-4296-9424-7 (paperback)
   ISBN 978-1-62065-331-9 (eBook PDF)
   1. Vegetables in human nutrition—Juvenile literature. I. Title.
   TX557.S383 2013
   641.5'636—dc23   2012009311

Information in this book supports
the U.S. Department of Agriculture's
MyPlate food guidance system found at
www.choosemyplate.gov. Food amounts
listed in this book are based on daily
recommendations for children ages 4–8.
The amounts listed in this book are
appropriate for children who get less than
30 minutes a day of moderate physical
activity, beyond normal daily activities.
Children who are more physically active
may be able to eat more while staying
within calorie needs. The U.S. Department
of Agriculture (USDA) does not endorse
any products, services, or organizations.

Editorial Credits
Jeni Wittrock, editor; Sarah Bennett, designer; Svetlana Zhurkin, media researcher; Kathy McColley,
   production specialist; Sarah Schuette, photo stylist; Marcy Morin, studio scheduler

Photo Credits
All photos by Capstone Studio/Karon Dubke except:
Shutterstock: Diana Taliun, cover, martascz, back cover; USDA, cover (inset), 5

The author dedicates this book to Rowan Grider of Milwaukee, Wisconsin.

Note to Parents and Teachers

The What's on MyPlate? series supports national science standards related to health and
nutrition. This book describes and illustrates MyPlate's vegetable recommendations. The images
support early readers in understanding the text. The repetition of words and phrases helps early
readers learn new words. This book also introduces early readers to subject-specific vocabulary
words, which are defined in the Glossary section. Early readers may need assistance to read
some words and to use the Table of Contents, Glossary, Read More, Internet Sites, and Index
sections of the book.

Printed in the United States of America in Eau Claire, Wisconsin.
052013   007407R

Table of Contents

MyPlate

Vegetables are a colorful part of MyPlate. MyPlate is a tool that helps you eat healthful food.

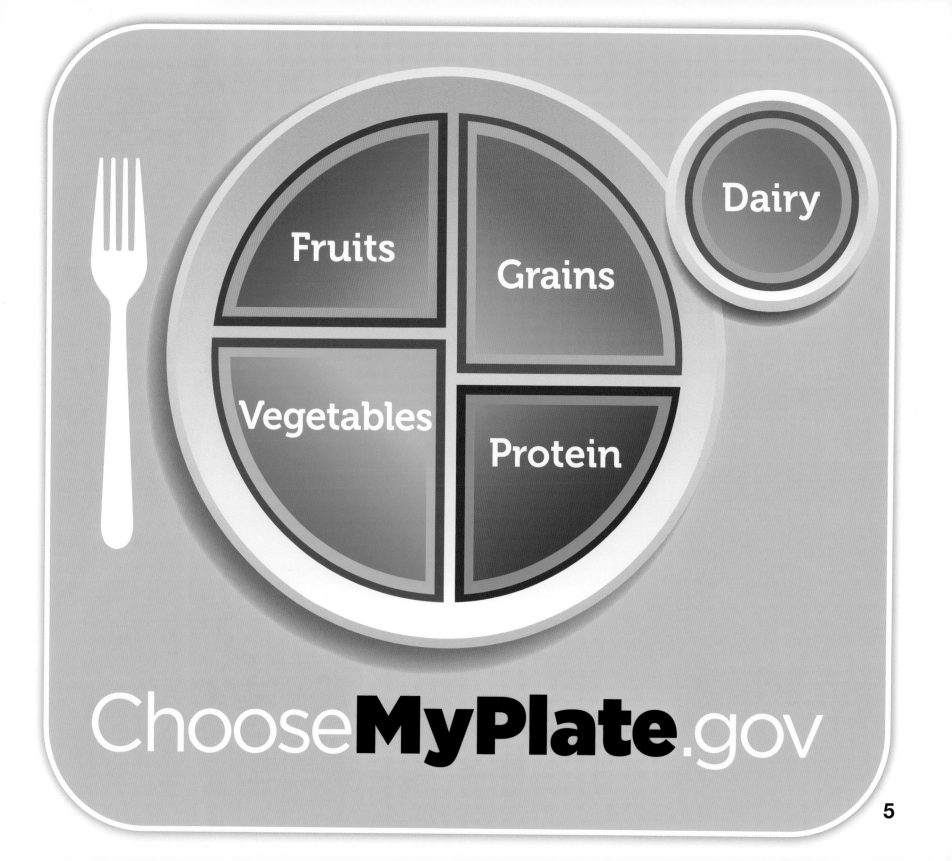

Fruits

Grains

Vegetables

Protein

Dairy

ChooseMyPlate.gov

Pass the peas, please!

Fill half your plate

with vegetables and fruit.

Each week, eat many kinds of vegetables. Every day kids should eat at least 1½ cups (360 milliliters) of vegetables.

All Kinds of Vegetables

Vegetables come from plants.

The nutrients in vegetables

keep you healthy and strong.

You can enjoy vegetables

in many ways.

Vegetables can be fresh,

canned, frozen, or dried.

Try different vegetables every day. Munch on squash, zucchini, and potatoes. There are so many vegetables to choose from!

Salads are full of vegetables.
Add cucumbers, carrots,
and spinach. See how many
colors you can eat.

Make a veggie pizza

with friends.

Top it with peppers, tomatoes,

and mushrooms.

Healthy Meals

You can add vegetables to other foods to make a heathful meal. What are your favorite vegetables?

How Much to Eat

Kids need to eat at least three servings of vegetables every day. To get three servings, pick three of your favorite vegetables below.

½ cup (120 mL)
broccoli

½ cup (120 mL)
carrots

½ cup (120 mL)
tomato juice

½ cup (120 mL) corn

½ baked potato

½ cup (120 mL)
green beans

½ cup (120 mL)
split peas

½ cup (120 mL)
kidney beans

Glossary

MyPlate—a food plan that reminds people to eat healthful food and be active; MyPlate was created by the U.S. Department of Agriculture

nutrient—something that people need to eat to stay healthy and strong; vitamins and minerals are nutrients

serving—one helping of food

vegetable—a part of a plant that people eat; vegetables can be roots, stems, leaves, flowers, or seeds

Read More

Aboff, Marcie. *The Incredible Vegetable Group.* MyPlate and Healthy Eating. Mankato, Minn.: Capstone Press, 2012.

Adams, Julia. *Vegetables.* Good Food. New York: PowerKids Press, 2011.

Dilkes, D. H. *Vegetables.* All about Good Foods We Eat. Berkeley Heights, N.J.: Enslow Elementary, 2012.

Internet Sites

FactHound offers a safe, fun way to find Internet sites related to this book. All of the sites on FactHound have been researched by our staff.

Here's all you do:

Visit *www.facthound.com*

Type in this code: 9781429687430

 Check out projects, games and lots more at **www.capstonekids.com**

Index

Word Count: 143
Grade: 1
Early-Intervention Level: 15

Vegetables are tasty, crunchy, and healthful. Learn about how MyPlate helps you make great food choices every day, including vegetables!

Everyone knows that when you eat right, you feel great. But what foods are best? How much of each kind of food do you need? Learn about MyPlate, a tool to help you eat better, and make every meal a healthful one.

TITLES IN THIS SET:

Dairy on MyPlate

Fruits on MyPlate

Get Moving!

Grains on MyPlate

Healthy Snacks on MyPlate

Protein on MyPlate

Sugars and Fats

Vegetables on MyPlate

RL: K-1   IL: PreK-2

ISBN 978-1-4296-9424-7

9 781429 694247   90000

Capstone Press®
a capstone imprint   www.capstonepub.com

T3-AIX-986